# SPEECHLESS

## Giving the #voiceless a Voice

Haakon mAncient Ueland
Charles Caldwell
Crystal Behe
Lafaya Mitchell
Sabrina Schottenhamel
Alecia C. Tolver
Lonnee Rey

**Lonnee Rey, Book Producer | Editor**

# CONTENTS

# FOREWORD

**Haakon mAncient Ueland**
Bachelor of Child Welfare (B.C.W.), Master of Child Welfare
Work student (M.C.W.W.), Doctor of Divinity (DD, hon.)

*"I am the voice of the voiceless; through me the dumb
shall speak. Till the deaf world's ears be made to
hear. The wrongs of the wordless weak." Ella Wheeler
Wilcox, poet.*

Have you ever been speechless?

When speech deserts a person, the resulting silence can ripple through their life like a stone cast into still waters. It may spring from the well of overwhelming emotions, where anxiety or fear grips the throat, leaving you stranded in a sea of unspoken words. In this quiet, relationships may falter, and isolation takes root, as the inability to express oneself becomes a barrier between the heart and the world. For some, it is not emotion but the mind itself that betrays them - neurological conditions steal their voice, casting shadows over once-clear thoughts. Whether fleeting or enduring, this loss of speech can erode confidence, deepen loneliness, and turn the vibrant tapestry of human connection into a muted echo of what once was.

It was Christmas 1982. My mum shouted "Come with me!"
I did.
TA was on the floor. "Grab his head!"
I did.
In spite of being a non-verbal autist, he made a sound. It gnawed on my heart, and a tear threatened to erupt from my eye. I held it back.
Five adults, or rather: four adults and one teen, holding him. Naked, he tried to rip off his penis.
We held him for an eternity.
Then he relaxed. Tears trailed down his face, wetting my hands.
On my mum's orders, we released him. She followed him into his bedroom, sat by his bedside. I watched, ready to step in if necessary.
His features smoothed out as he fell asleep.

~

When I first met TA, it was spring. Running through a huge garden, a devil-may-care smile on his handsome teen face, he seemed as free as a deer.
TA lived in an institution for autistic men and children. Until four, his development was normal. Then he changed. According to his dad, after a vaccine.
Non-verbal, he spoke through actions. Sometimes, he hurt himself. Other times, us.
Looking into his eyes was akin to seeing into the Pacific. Sky blue all the way down.

~

The rules of his world were complex. Peas and carrots should never be mixed. New clothes could lead to hours of problematic behavior. Before opening a door, the handle had to be tapped four times. Self-inflicted pain was no problem. Accidents made him cry.

~

Fast forward a few years. TA had gotten a language, a simplified version of sign language. His days were meticulously planned, using a huge clock with symbols signifying activities of daily life. He enjoyed long rides on our tandem cycle, enjoying the wind hitting his face.

We went to Greece and Spain. He put his face under the surface of swimming pools, and could stay there longer than we could.

We had tested gluten- and lactose-free food, but it made no difference. What mattered to him was that his life went according to plan. That he was allowed to live life on his terms.

~

I meet him occasionally, having worked with him for 10 years. In 2017, a few months after my mother had transitioned from this world, I met him again. I told him that he would not meet Reidun anymore. I also told him that she often spoke of him . That he was important in her life.

In the ten years I worked with him, I had seen him in various states. I had never experienced him looking straight into my eyes for minutes before. My mother was reflected in his eyes.

His angelic smile as I left linger in my heart.

To help someone who is voiceless, you can offer support in simple yet meaningful ways. First, use non-verbal communication tools like gestures, facial expressions, or visual aids such as communication boards or picture-based systems to help them express their needs and feelings more easily. Second, be patient and give them the time they need to communicate without rushing or interrupting, as this fosters a calm environment and reduces their stress. Lastly, respect their autonomy by asking how they prefer to communicate and offering choices when appropriate, ensuring they feel empowered and included in the conversation.

At the root, realizing that someone is voiceless is the beginning of making a change in another. This book will help you. In this short read, you will meet different examples of being speechless: A beauty pageant family that doesn't accept alternate life choices; an introvert that became a Toastmaster; a poker player who turned pain into healing, two men who chose to die before their voices faded, a daughter's love/hate story that inspired her to create a legacy of better communication with her children, and a best friend who passed but whose messages of love, family and forgiveness will live on.

**Haakon Rian Mancient Ueland** is a Norwegian social worker, healer, father of three, and grandfather of two. With a bachelor's degree in Child Welfare Work, he has dedicated his life to helping others.

Ueland is also a Tulku (reincarnated lama) and monk of his own denomination (Earth House Church). He is certified in various healing modalities, including Tsa Lung and Holistic Healing, and is recognised as a Star Matrix Master. He is a bestselling international writer thanks to Editor Lonnee Rey.

As an artist known as **mAncient**, Ueland creates healing music that resonates with a large online following. His mission is to make the world a better place for future generations, traveling with his dog, Trollheads Nessi, to spread his message of compassion and healing.

# HAAKON RIAN MANCIENT UELAND
## ... FEATHERS BURNT BY DEMENTIA

**Gollum**

Have you seen Lord of the Rings?

T was Gollum personified. Hunched over, no hair, bony and small ... but most of all, his eyes. Dark with pain.

"Håkon! You came! Come in - I have coffee!!!"

"My dog is in the car. May I bring him in?"

"Of course. I have been thinking of getting a new dog. A doberman like Chuck."

This statement was repeated every time he saw my Cooper Frost.

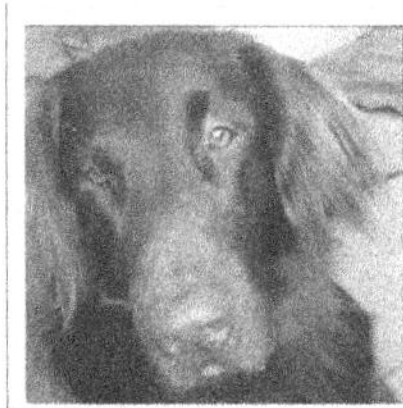

Cooper Frost

T was my mother's ex-partner. Their relationship was stormy, ranging from burning love to violence.

Twice, violent when I was present. Twice, I had to intervene. The last time was the beginning of the end for their relationship.

T was a former Marinejeger (Navy Seal) and had won gold in a Norwegian junior boxing championship.

Strong and wiry, quick as a viper.

When drunk, he sometimes got mellow. Sometimes mean.

This was mean. He had had hard liquor - lots. Sitting between my mum and me in the small farm where they lived, he grabbed a crystal glass and took a bite.

The sound of him chewing was painful.
Then he struck my mum. Fist to face. While looking at me.
I grabbed him, threw him over the coffee table, jumped over it, and put him in a chokehold.
All the bruises and her "accidents" weighed on my heart.
"A little more pressure, and he will not hurt her again" flew through my mind as I asked her to call the police.
He wiggled.
"Just a little more pressure."
A quiet cry erupted.
"NO! THIS IS NOT WHO I AM!"
I kept holding him in a chokehold, adding an arm-lock.
"It hurts, Haakon! Let me up! I am calm!"
"We will wait until the police arrive, T. Just relax."
Never had blue flashing lights felt so good.
Handcuffed, he was taken away.
Soon thereafter, the farm was sold, and mum split the proceeds with him. In his favor.

~

He had visited her a few times since then. The last time was not successful. He got drunk on the train from Sweden to Norway, provoked a fight, and got beat up.
He didn't stay long.
When she died, we called him. He didn't come to her funeral.

~

With alcohol-induced dementia, an unhealed throat after the removal of a cancerous tumor, and memories that sucked his life juice, he was not in a good place.
With 22 years of social work, I have seen a lot of misery. This was the pinnacle.
He had lost contact with his daughter. One of his brothers, Runar, took advantage of his dementia, and bled him dry

financially. Silently approved by his other brother.
I was on my way to a spiritual Ayahuasca-retreat in Sweden, and promised I would return.

~

When I did, T invited me to stay. Recently divorced, with a bank account full of cash and no immediate plans, I agreed. So we moved in: my dog Cooper, whom I had trained as a therapy dog since he was eight weeks, my keyboards and me.
T was the most challenging client I have ever worked with. His reactivity was second to none. In spite of his dementia, he was highly observant of slights, and the deep hurt that festered in his mind was abrasive to an empath such as myself.

~

One month after I moved in, I discovered why people looked at him with suspicion tinged with fear. He was known as "the crazy Norwegian who killed his dog with a knife and who pulls out his own teeth."
I spoke with him about what had happened. He told me that he could no longer control the dog. What he said, under the surface, was that he also planned to leave this plane himself. But he had a change of heart. Or … forgot it.

For three months we worked together. Sang together. He showed me how to play steel guitar - he was one of the few Norwegians who played on the stage of the Grand Ole Opry. We spoke about his nightly travels; he told me that he was very often tired when waking up, as he traveled to problematic places in the world to fix whatever a warrior could fix.
He had his teeth fixed, after I got him an appointment with a dentist. A month after I came, he went for his first walk alone with my dog .

And we started the process of healing his relationship with his daughter, whom I was very happy to hear visited him after I left.

It was exhausting. I took frequent trips to Norway, and long walks in the forest, to vent my overworked mind.

As his strength increased, so did his memory. He asked me to get his boxing bag from a neighbor, as he wanted to box. He shared his suspicions that his brothers had cheated him in the settlement after the death of his mother.

That was the beginning of the end. He had meticulous notes and records of his finances, and I agreed that there seemed to be something fishy.

Three times a day, home-aids came with food for him. One of them suggested that he should get a guardian. We spoke about it, and he said yes, but only if I would do it.

I disagreed. In Sweden, this task is divided into three: help with controlling finances and paying bills, help with daily activities such as grocery shopping, and overseeing everything related to the client. I suggested that I would do the last part, and that his neighbor would continue doing the first two.

We sent in an application. No response for a long while. He was adamant that he wanted me to be a part of it, otherwise he would withdraw his consent.

The papers from the court came. They had appointed a lawyer, and he was furious.

~

I had met a girl; the last relationship I had before becoming a monk in 2019. She was Norwegian, so I had some extended stays in Norway.

One day, I got a message from him. His brother, the one whom he suspected had taken advantage of him, said that I had to move out. That if I didn't "get all my sh*t out" before

the end of the week, it would all be thrown out on the lawn.
So I moved back to Norway.

~

He called me some time later. Shortly before he died. He had
moved to Norway, and wanted me to come visit.
I was too late.

~

*I heard from his daughter some time after his passing. She, too,
suspected that his brother had bled him dry. The executor of his
will agreed. But … it was difficult to prove. So Runar got away
with it.*
*May Karma hit him hard.*

◆ ◆ ◆

If you could write a poem (to TA)
by Haakon Rian mAncient Ueland

If you could write a poem,
I wonder what you'd write,
A poem filled with joyfulness
or sorrow, fear and fright

I look into your dark eyes
and know not what I see
Is there a part of me in there,
or is it only me

If you could write a poem,
I bet my final dime,
I couldn't really read it,
your time is not my time

Your dreams are universal,
you find them everywhere,
some find it in their music,

some find it in despair

If you could write a poem,
I wonder what you'd write,
A poem filled with loneliness,
or birds in distant flight

If you could write a poem,
I really wish you could
I'd read it with my heart and soul
I'd read it with my blood

If you could write a poem,
I wouldn't know what to do
Should I then give it to the world
or give it back to you

Your dreams are universal,
they come from love and fear
If you could write a poem,
I'd read it if I dare

Your poem might be fire,
My poem might be snow
Our poems are a part of us
We write them as we go

If you could write a poem,
the poem of your life
I'd read it with my heart and soul
I'd read it in the night

I'd read it with my heart and soul
I'd read it in the night.
(https://audius.co/mAncient_one/if-you-could-
write-a-poem - vocals and steel by T)

*"Christ asked people who followed him to be the voice for the voiceless- not to wire their mouths shut."* Christina Engela, indie writer.

**Haakon Rian Mancient Ueland** is a Norwegian social worker, healer, father of three, and grandfather of two. With a bachelor's degree in Child Welfare Work, he has dedicated his life to helping others.

Ueland is also a Tulku (reincarnated lama) and monk of his own denomination (Earth House Church). He is certified in various healing modalities, including Tsa Lung and Holistic Healing, and is recognised as a Star Matrix Master. He is a bestselling international writer thanks to Editor Lonnee Rey.

As an artist known as **mAncient**, Ueland creates healing music that resonates with a large online following. His mission is to make the world a better place for future generations, traveling with his dog to spread his message of compassion and healing.

For public speaking or consulting inquiries:
- LinkedIn: www.linkedin.com/in/mancient
- Email: mancient@protonmail.com
- WhatsApp: +47 99 567 564

More info:
- Earth House Church: www.earthhouse.church
- Star Matrix Master: www.goe.ac
- Music: www.mancient.com

# CHARLES CALDWELL … DON'T BE AFRAID TO GROW OLD

*"We don't grow old. When we cease to grow, we become old." — Ralph Waldo Emerson*

We relate to our parents as the air that we breathe, and when that air disappears, when a parent passes away, it is a big shock to the system. It is like sucking oxygen from our lungs,…the very oxygen that sucked the life from my parents when the time came. Metaphysically, it is a shock to our personal safety, our comfort zone and life.

In the summer of 2018, a shadow fell over my wife's family when my father-in-law, Blake, was diagnosed with Alzheimer's disease. Only in his mid-70s, he seemed too vibrant for such a fate. Initially, he masked his struggles with forgetfulness, wielding humor like a shield against the encroaching darkness. Blake was known for his incredible sense of humor, effortlessly transforming even the dullest moments into comedy gold, making us laugh so hard we often forgot what we were worried about in the first place. Playing "Cards Against Humanity" with Blake guaranteed you a night of hilarity and joy.

But beneath the laughter, we sensed an unsettling truth: something was undeniably wrong. As we navigated this new reality, we were forced to confront not just Blake's battle, but our own perceptions of aging, memory, and the essence of what it truly means to grow.

Blake was deeply worried that this disease would lead him to cease growing, and in that cessation, he would truly grow old. Years earlier in his twenties, Blake had witnessed a handful of his relative's heartbreaking struggles with dementia, where they ultimately lost recognition of everyone around them. This led Blake to decide that if he faced the same fate, he would choose to die early rather than endure the perceived indignities of the diagnosis. Determined to avoid that road, Blake made a courageous choice early on: he opted for Death With Dignity, also known as Medical Assistance in Dying (MAID).

This decision was not an act of surrender but a powerful declaration of his desire to maintain control over his life and death, allowing him to face the end with dignity and free from the fear of losing both his physical and mental faculties. As he explained, he wasn't afraid of MAID itself but was afraid of what would happen if he didn't pursue it. In his quest for growth, even in darkness, Blake sought to define the terms of his existence, embodying Emerson's belief that we must strive to grow, no matter the circumstances. One of Blake's famous pieces of advice was to "pick your battles," and the battle with Alzheimer's was one he was cautiously navigating.

We all have family members who have passed on, and my story is not necessarily more special than yours. But if these words can inspire you to remember the legacies of your own loved ones, to reflect anew, or even to consider your own legacy, then it is worth sharing. As Henry David Thoreau noted, death can inspire us to become our better selves, urging us to live with responsibility and respect for those we've lost. Embracing this perspective helps us overcome the fear of ageing. In my father's words, "Don't be afraid to grow old."

~

My wife's family had about fifteen months' warning as Blake approached his choice. Planning for the procedure involved multiple consultations with physicians, and it was crucial for Blake to confirm his decision before Alzheimer's progressed beyond a certain point - often described as the "ten to twelve" mark on a clock. Beyond this stage, the medical and legal community would argue that he no longer had the mental capacity to consent to the procedure.

In September 2019, fifteen months after Blake's initial diagnosis and amidst escalating social unrest in Hong Kong, I followed my wife Tess to Canada to support Blake and the family during his final days. I arrived in sunny Kelowna on a Thursday afternoon before driving two hours north to Salmon Arm. I was greeted with a surreal atmosphere, everyone was aware Blake had a scheduled departure: Saturday at 3 PM and the countdown was on.

Blake was not afraid to grow old. He viewed Death with Dignity as a service to others, not wanting to be a burden or nuisance as the disease took its toll on his mind and body. A frugal man, he danced with joy whenever he found a penny on the ground, and nothing would upset him more than a disease robbing him of his hard-earned money. He decided he would not let that happen, which is why he chose his path, displaying incredible courage in the process. My role, as I saw it, was not to judge but to love Blake and his family. Little did I know that it would be Blake and his family who would teach me the true act of love.

At the time, I was an active Deacon (Elder) at Union Church Hong Kong, a multi-denominational English-speaking church. When I shared the situation regarding MAID, I secretly hoped they might remove me from the Deacons Court for ethical reasons and relieve me of my church duties. Instead, they echoed my belief: our role is to love one another, not to cast judgment. (And I was so close to a clean getaway!)

Although Blake believed in God, he saw Christ as a historical figure rather than a divine one. But as Nicky Gumbel said in The Alpha Course, "We never know the last thoughts of a dying man who utters a prayer immediately before a fatal car accident," or feels a paralytic overcoming his body. Even more so, God is omnipresent, exists across time, and has an infinity to answer our prayers.

Our job is to love one another, especially when family or friends seek support. A friend of mine went through a painful divorce, the circumstances of which could make it hard for people to support him. He confided in me that when he turned to other friends for comfort and an appeal for help, one told him, "You're right; you are sick. You need help. Go get professional help because I can't assist you." He was deeply hurt by this comment. I did my best to support him and love him despite the circumstances.

Blake was easy to love. This was universally agreed. I confess at times I found his choice of Death with Dignity sometimes difficult to understand. I often found myself questioning, "My gosh, what on earth is happening? Have you really thought this through?" Ultimately, however, my commitment was to love and support Blake, ensuring that our last days together would be filled with love, dignity, and respect.

When I arrived in Salmon Arm, I encountered a dynamic akin to a trinity of love, celebration, and apprehension. The apprehension emanated from no one desiring Blake's impending death. The love came from a deep respect and admiration for him. The celebration came from knowing that we had limited time, and that we were going to make the most of it. This family knew how to party, too. Blake, the first to pour a drink, would mix himself a rye and ginger then quickly forget he had done so while making another. They sat all over the house like little liquid easter eggs. As Saturday approached, the family engaged in robust celebrations, filling the home with joy. I initially expected a somber mood, but instead and despite the apprehension of what was about to happen, it was filled with respect, love, and a spirited celebration that my wife's family embraced wholeheartedly.

Each meal that we shared together featured a question. For instance, we would ask, "What is your favorite memory of Blake?" or "What was your funniest moment with him?" Everyone would take turns sharing their cherished memories and anecdotes. This tradition continued over the several days leading up to Saturday, adding to the celebration.

The day after I arrived in Salmon Arm, we arranged Zoom calls between Blake and our four teenagers back in Hong Kong. Each teen had one-on-one time with Blake, providing a chance to say goodbye. They shared a close relationship with Blake, filled with fond memories from trips to the Philippines, Hong Kong, Europe, and the United

States, as well as annual gatherings at Fintry on Lake Okanagan. Despite the impending loss, they maintained their composure with their grandfather, who was still very much himself and made them laugh and cry. While they were emotional, they had taken the time to plan ahead what they wanted to say: thoughtful statements made the conversations meaningful, heartfelt and memorable.

This was a remarkable aspect of the MAID experience. The opportunity to say goodbye and share last words is invaluable, but it is not always possible when someone is facing an imminent death from a terminal illness, for example. Often, individuals in that situation are suffering and experiencing mental fatigue or "end-of-life confusion," which can hinder meaningful communication. The opportunity may disappear altogether if the death is sudden.

In Blake's situation, he was mostly very much himself, sharp and engaged. This allowed the kids - and all of us - to have meaningful, rational conversations with him. We were able to express our gratitude for everything he had done for the family, which was considerable.

Many people were calling to give Blake their last farewell. This included my father, who called to have a private conversation with Blake. They shared a great friendship; although they didn't speak often, their conversations were always filled with laughter. My father once sent Blake a birthday card that Blake repeatedly recalled as the funniest piece of mail he'd ever received.

I encouraged Dad to call Blake, sensing it was important for them to connect. When he did call, I promptly went to find Blake, having already informed him to expect the call.

As I handed the phone to Blake, I felt a strong urge to eavesdrop on their conversation. However, I decided against it, wanting to maintain the integrity of the moment. I closed the bedroom door and let them talk. I would find out months later what they discussed.

Blake wrote "last letters" to all his family members, some of whom received multiple letters because he forgot to whom he had written.

I had a GoPro and recorded much of the last few days - walks, meals, and many meaningful moments - resulting in several gigabytes of footage. I also had the opportunity to spend private time with Blake, asking him life questions and capturing his messages for others. He was incredibly generous with his time. One memorable thing Blake once told me: "No matter how angry you are, never withhold love from a child."

My commitment to preserving stories began after my mother passed away years ago. I realized that many family stories were slowly being lost over time. When I sensed my mother's health declining, I wanted to capture her story on video, but I never had the chance. This motivated me to document the lives of others in similar situations. I first did this with my wife's grandparents, recording an hour of them sharing their experiences as a young couple during World War II and reflecting on their long lives together.

During those last few days with Blake, we visited some of his favorite places, like the breakfast spots he loved. People were genuinely excited to see him and the whole family together, including the spouses of his children.

I remember one particular breakfast on the "last Saturday

morning" when Blake quietly mentioned to a waitress he knew, "By the way, this is the last time I'll be seeing you." It was shocking for some, but it allowed them a moment of closure - which is often absent in sudden deaths and not always guaranteed in terminal illnesses.

Charles & Blake
The morning of...

One of the positive aspects of MAID was the ability to prepare. In addition to my recordings, my wife's sister arranged for a professional photographer to capture family photos on our last morning together. Knowing what was approaching allowed us to plan for what we thought would be important: capturing pictures, recording videos, and sharing stories and laughter - keepsakes for the future.

Our last evening together, we all sat playing Blake's favourite songs, many of which were golden oldies. He and Maureen, my mother-in-law, danced, we shared stories, laughter, and poignant moments, but no one cried. All of this was captured on video.

Finally, Saturday arrived. Tess read her favorite childhood storybook to Blake. We took the last pictures. The IV nurse arrived to insert the IV stent so that this would be taken care of ahead of time.

The plan was to walk to the funeral home where the procedure would take place. "We'll save money," Blake exclaimed, "if I die at the funeral home!" There was concern about being late and we started to get separated from one another as we walked. I stopped everyone and explained we had to walk together, "This is one time when you really do want to stop and smell the roses."

The funeral home had a very comfortable room prepared with one of Blake's favorite comfy chairs brought down from the house earlier. The attending physician went through last-minute legalities, triple-checking that Blake's choice was MAID. The IV nurse entered the room to hand the medication to the physician: giant syringes that looked as though they were filled with milk, water and fruit punch.

We all gathered around next to Blake who said a few final words of appreciation. The family responded with messages of encouragement and love. Without getting into the specific medicines, basically here is what happens: Blake was given a powerful sedative that made him fall asleep. A coma-inducing medication was administered followed by a paralytic that stopped the lungs. Eventually, the heart stops. Between the three major drugs, lesser drugs and saline flushes are quickly used to ensure there are no complications or discomfort from the main drugs interacting with one another along the way. Blake fell asleep, he lost some color, and his lips turned blue. The time of death was declared. The whole procedure lasted maybe 6-7 minutes, if that. The physician and IV nurse excused themselves. It was all over.

But that wasn't the point.

From the moment Blake began to drift away, for those six to seven minutes, Blake's family showered him with a level of love and encouragement I had never witnessed before. Maureen crouched atop Blake, holding his cheeks in her hands, speaking warmth, hope, and love into the heart of the one she cherished, reminding him that he was not alone. On that day, Blake's family taught me the true meaning of love.

I'm not sure what was more transformative: witnessing Blake's passing through MAID or watching his family shower him with love. You see, this was not the norm for me; I was more the conservative, reserved type. In my family, love was expressed not through affirmation or words, but through acts of service. We didn't always say "I love you"; instead, we expressed it in subtler ways, like asking about the weather or doing favors. One way we say "I love you" is through the expression "Boil the Water," which originated when one of my sisters spent two and a half years working in a developing country, where there were constant concerns about her falling ill due to poor infrastructure and sanitation. Fast forward to modern times in Canada, and my family excels at airport pick-ups - another way we show our love.

I sat there, watching this extraordinary scene unfold. Blake's death inspired me to want to live fully and make the most of every moment. Those six or seven minutes were beautiful, despite their tragic nature. As the minutes passed, Blake's family gathered themselves, exchanging a few words about who was going where, who was walking and who needed a ride, when would we all gather back at the house. Slowly we departed, profusely thanking the staff as we left. What we didn't know was that outside waiting for us was Grief.

That evening, as we assembled back at the house, the mood began to shift from celebration to mourning. As the party continued we searched everywhere in the house, and not a single rye and ginger, no matter how many days old, was left unconsumed. Over the next few days, there was a private cremation and, as per Blake's request, his ashes were kept in a large Skippy Extra Smooth peanut butter jar.

Tess and I returned to Hong Kong, believing that life would resume as normal. While the social unrest settled down, it was soon replaced by a once-in-a-lifetime global pandemic. I also thought that Blake and MAID marked the end of the Death with Dignity story. I began writing the first half of this chapter in the ensuing months, preparing to share it as a talk at the Christian Men's Fellowship Lunch in January 2020. However, I encountered writer's block and also grief that greeted me unexpectedly, like an uninvited guest, at inopportune moments - when I was on a bus, say. I felt as though the story had no conclusion. Indeed, it turns out the story was far from finished with much more to unfold. God had other plans.

*If you want to change the world, go home and*
*love your family* – Mother Teresa

L et me share a bit about myself. My story revolves around holding onto the past too much, much like Gatsby. Throughout my life, I've raced against time, striving to stay one step ahead and cling to my youth. If you follow me on social media, you'll know that in recent years, I've focused on losing weight, training, and running faster - not just for the love of competition, but out of a desire to retain my youth. Death occasionally reminded me of its inevitable presence, often feeling like an approaching defeat. However, as I grew older, any loneliness I felt dissipated, and I found myself traveling many wonderful roads.

Over the past twenty years at Union Church and in other Christian communities, I've learned the profound power of fellowship, known in Greek as Koinonia. Proverbs 27:17 states, "As iron sharpens iron, so one person sharpens another." My Christian men's group has been vital in keeping me grounded; we share our joys, burdens, secrets, and concerns. I know I can always reach out to this micro-community for prayer and support, helping me stay attuned to God's leading.

Never underestimate the importance of family, community, and fellowship. I was fortunate to have parents who provided my sisters and me with an incredible upbringing filled with adventure - skiing, sailing, and access to a great education. My father taught me much about using tools of all kinds, building and repairing things, making wine, and first aid. The lessons were endless and he had many valuable expressions such as: "measure twice, cut once" and "work hard, save your money."

1962 Dad & Baby Charles

(Holding me as a baby during a visit to Antigua)

My dad was very conscious that his adult years and career coincided with a time of tremendous economic expansion and prosperity in the post-World War II era - something that many generations may not experience again for some time. Our strong family unit was a cornerstone of my upbringing. Looking back, I realize that I may have been a bit difficult at the time, ungrateful for those lessons, but I appreciate them in hindsight.

One of my powerful early memories is of my family's sailing trip to the Bahamas when I was only five years old. One night while anchored off a quiet shore in remote Bahamas, we dragged our anchor during a sudden and unexpected midnight storm. Chaos erupted. My father and my older sisters, in the slashing rain and inky darkness, leapt onto the deck to save our 28-foot sailboat as it rushed toward the coral. I remember the storm pitching our little boat back and forth and my father yelling down to my mother, "Don't let Charles look outside."

Of course, as a little five-year-old, No WAY would I go back to my bunk and sleeping bag. I was determined to look outside! My mother was illuminating the scene with a powerful beamlight, and I will never forget looking outside, through the cabin's hatch, and seeing devastation just a heartbeat away. We were so close to the rocks but I had NO fear. I knew that under my father's loving arms, and my mother's care, I was okay. I was excited about life and what lay ahead… what an amazing adventure my life was with my family.

Charles & Dad / Doug
Father's Day

For the next 50+ years, that was my father's life… always striving for the next horizon or secure anchorage and leading the rest of us on that journey.

Like Blake, my mother passed away very young, at 72. After her death, my dad went through a period of darkness, but he emerged determined to live his best life. He faced the long and painful process of selling a family country property called "Marblehill" a few hours north of Toronto. It was named after an area in Antigua where my mother had grown up. Marblehill had accumulated decades of antiques and collectables. All of that had to go. Next came the task of downsizing the house where I was raised. I was living in Hong Kong and unable to be of any help, but my two sisters worked tirelessly to support my father in wrapping up these two properties. Eventually, Dad moved into a perfect condo in a cozy part of downtown Toronto that was close to all his favorite things. He began creating the best life ever.

For almost two decades, my father embarked on one adventure after another. He visited Hong Kong at least twice, and we traveled to Shanghai together.

I flew him down for my MBA graduation at Northwestern University. He explored all sorts of interesting places around the world and, oh yes, he sailed - locally around Lake Ontario and with friends who were off on their own sailing voyages around the world, joining them for two to three weeks at a time.

Charles & Dad / Doug
(At a family wedding)

Meanwhile, when at home, Dad cooked and baked (often contributing cookies to Sunday church services), entertained regularly in his new home, became a great-grandfather, and even learned to play the ukulele writing an original song entitled, "Don't Be Afraid To Grow Old."

A few months after Blake passed away, in early 2020, my father fell ill after having been in and out of the hospital a few times in previous years. While protests in Hong Kong had subsided, another adversary - COVID - reared its ugly head, bringing travel restrictions, quarantines, and the necessity of isolation. It was early in the pandemic, long before vaccines were available and even before COVID testing for travel was deemed necessary.

Meanwhile, my father's health was deteriorating, and he was hospitalized again. Due to COVID, his hospital stay was incredibly lonely; no visitors were allowed, and he spent weeks alone. To make matters worse, the protocols varied based on different ailments, often contradicting one another depending on whether he tested positive for COVID or not. This was also before rapid antigen tests. He had to undergo COVID testing, which seemed to take days to get the results back before any potential treatments could be considered.

Eventually, the doctors diagnosed him, and in short, his body was starting to give out. While he wasn't afraid of growing old, the reality was that at 92 years old, his body was calling it quits. The general medical consensus was that, if he was lucky, he might have six months to live, perhaps up to 18 months. But everyone knew he might not last more than a few weeks. My father expressed a desire to return home. My sisters and I supported his decision, understanding he probably would never return to the hospital. We arranged 24-hour care to look after him.

The question remained: would I go back to Canada? With Hong Kong in near-total lockdown and cases surging in Canada, I found myself contemplating the trip. This is where my community came into play. I reached out to my men's group asking for prayer. I shared my doubts about returning, leaning toward staying put. Traveling would mean putting myself and my family at risk. At that point, no one knew much about COVID. My only reference was SARS, which Tess and I experienced in 2003-2004. Even though the SARS mortality rate ended up being only 11%, there was a time when it approached 50%.

However, my Christian brothers had a different perspective. I remember one of them texting in the group chat, "Whoa, whoa, whoa... Okay, wait, hold on a second here."

Through prayer with my family and discussions with my brothers, I realized there was no alternative but to return to Canada. It struck me that this was a leadership moment. My father was there when I was born, and his parents were with him when he was born. Who should be with him when he dies? Who should be with me when I die? These thoughts circulated in my mind, reminding me of Mother Teresa's words: "If you want to change the world, go home and love your family." My place was with my family during this time.

How certain was I that my father was going to die? Perhaps this would just be another hospital visit, and he'd be off sailing again in a few months. The answer was clear: my father was physically uncomfortable to the point of embarrassment. As a physician, he could read between the lifelines.

Then, my father sprang a big surprise. While Blake gave his family over a year's warning about his decision to end his life via Dying With Dignity, my father informed my sisters and me with only a few weeks' notice. This decision was not surrendering or fear of growing old - he was already old. It stemmed from his desire to maintain control over his life and death, allowing him to face the end with dignity and without fear of losing his body on its terms.

I later learned what Blake and my father discussed during that pivotal phone call. My dad told Blake how brave he thought he was and expressed his respect for Blake's decision. They talked about the ethical considerations surrounding medical assistance in dying, a topic people often wrestle with. My father's support for Blake was something I hadn't known at the time, and it wasn't until my father disclosed his own wishes that I fully understood the significance of their conversation.

It made sense now: my father was an anaesthetist who dealt with life-and-death situations throughout his career. For example, he stabilized motorcycle accident victims on life support for organ donation more than once, and sat on several ethics committees. The concept of medical assistance in dying was not new to him, and now he would be a willing participant.

I quickly made preparations to return to Canada, including getting a COVID blood test (the only test available at that point) at my own expense. At least in Hong Kong, they were efficient, and I had the results in two hours. (Though authorities, for example, didn't seem to care: "A COVID test? Who cares! You're coming from Hong Kong. You MUST be infected!") But seriously, by the time I boarded the plane, I understood why God was sending me back. It wasn't just to go home and love my family; it was also to practice the lessons learned from Blake's family.

The days leading up to my father's passing were, in some ways, similar to Blake's, and in others, quite different. The process of choosing MAID was much faster because my father's body was physically failing him. The physical assessment was easy whereas with Blake it was more of a mental assessment. But unlike Blake, there was no partying; my father's body was too weak and he simply couldn't celebrate like it was 1999. We took plenty of pictures and even videos of him playing the ukulele, but at that point, having a professional photographer felt inappropriate. Years earlier, I had already videoed my father sharing stories about his journeys and his reflections on life.

People did call and several visited. Tess and the kids video-called Dad, and once again, they had thoughtfully prepared what they wanted to say. One visitor, in particular, brought champagne, and they shared a private celebration together. That person left in tears and, three years later, chose MAID after being diagnosed with ALS.

Each evening, my father might have a small scotch or a touch of wine, and whoever wasn't the designated driver would join him. But the libations didn't flow as freely as they did with Blake's family; my father's body was much frailer. Each situation is unique in those final days, and you have to meet people where they are.

Like Blake, my dad received wonderful, loving messages from people he reached out to. People called, and my father made phone calls as well. One of the most touching phone calls came from Maureen who told my father, "Your journey will be safe."

The day arrived, and as before everything felt a little surreal. But this time there was no walking or stopping to smell the roses - my father was already somewhat bedridden. We gathered ourselves, and when the physician arrived, an IV stent was inserted. My sisters and I were left alone with our father. It was only minutes now until the end.

We thanked him for everything under the sun and told him how much we loved him: a great life, wonderful grandkids, family, and great opportunities. My father replied, "It was all your mother's fault."

I asked if he wanted me to pray, and he said, "If you like." So typical. We had shared many philosophical conversations about life, Christianity, and God. While he attended church regularly, he kept his convictions close to his chest. I prayed Psalm 23 over him, inserting his name throughout: "The Lord is Doug's shepherd..." and so on. As we approached the end, my father spoke the last words of the Psalm with me: "and I will dwell in the house of the Lord forever."

"Yes, you will," I said.

A few minutes later, the doctor entered my father's bedroom. There they were... THE syringes. I felt my conservative self recoil in horror. But I knew why I was there. I felt the Lord urging me to rise up. The three of us stood together, holding my father's hands and each other, speaking warmth, hope, and love into the heart of the one we cherished, reminding him he was not alone.

In the end, it truly was death with dignity, and it was a profound privilege to witness it while God showed me how to love in a whole new way.

We should not fret, for we are safe. Our mothers, fathers, and loved ones are always there for us. They are not speechless; they live on in the wonderful, loving stories we share. My father was not afraid to grow old, and when the time came, he sailed off gracefully.

**It was a beautiful ending as my father spoke his last words: "It's a victory, not defeat."**

**Charles Caldwell** is on a mission to demonstrate love as a leadership skill. Committed to many youth causes, he believes that "My

Even Blake's obituary had people dying of laughter.

Read the log of Doug's final voyage.

ceiling is the next generation's floor." Originally from Canada, Charles has lived in Hong Kong for 28 years, where he balances his career as a senior HR professional with being a husband and father of four, including triplets. The constant searchlight of insight, he inspires others to take action and realize their potential. His calm presence serves as a steady anchor, guiding leaders through challenges and opportunities alike. Charles is happiest when, at the end of a journey, leaders look back and say, "We did it ourselves."

Reach out to him for help with complex HR issues, mentoring, or executive and leadership coaching, to experience his dedication to empowering the next generation of leaders. You can find Charles on LinkedIn here https://www.linkedin.com/in/charlesbdcaldwell/ and explore more about him here. linktr.ee/charlescaldwell.

# CRYSTAL BEHE ... TOSS THE CROWN, EMBRACE THE CLAWS

Did you ever feel like you didn't fit in, no matter how hard you tried? All you ever wanted was to find your place in this world, your tribe where you could be you. Why is it so important to fit into the box that your family and society want you to fit in? Growing up, I only had one person in my life who bucked the system in every way and followed her heart no matter what. I want to share her message with you, proving that you are not alone, that tribe is there for you, and being true to yourself is what matters most ... the rest will come. Above all, protect the ones you love with all your heart, including yourself.

~

My pageant family pic:
10 yo Susan, left – Sandy, right

Growing up in a beauty pageant household was like living in a world of polished perfection, where every detail—from how we looked to how we acted—was under a microscope. Our mom's rules about dieting, rehearsing interview speeches, and spending hours making sure our hair looked flawless were as strict as they were exhausting. But my sister Susan? She was always different. At fifteen, she finally decided to break free from that mold, leaving behind the pageants to explore who she was outside of Mom's carefully curated world. Unlike our sister Sandy, Susan didn't have that perfect pageant smile or drive, and she wasn't interested in being model-thin or as academically focused. She didn't belong in that world—and she didn't want to.

There's a 20-year gap between us, so a lot of her story happened before I was born. But I grew up hearing about how, in the early '80s in West Davie, our family home was a place where appearances were everything. Mom would have each of us practice posing in front of mirrors, making sure we stood up straight, held our shoulders back, and smiled "just so." But Susan? She had her own way of doing things. She'd roll her eyes when Mom wasn't looking or sneak me a cookie whenever she had the chance. She didn't just dislike the pageant world; she actively rejected it. She liked what society sometimes labeled "wrong"— she preferred boys' clothes, listened to music classified as "black music," and even dated black guys, a decision that wasn't well-received back then. Her determination to be herself, despite everything, became an example for me to live authentically.

When I was little, Susan wasn't around much. Mom worried about her being a "bad influence," but I was fascinated by her boldness whenever I got to see her. Susan was loud and fun, refusing to take crap from anyone, but she was also caring and kind as long as others were kind to her. She was Daddy's girl, through and through, but our dad—"Papa," as I called him—was away working a lot as a yacht captain, so he wasn't around to protect her from Mom's vision of what we should be. Susan lived her life unapologetically, and before she passed, she told me,

"Always protect your kids and let them be whoever they want to be. Love them freely." Her words have stayed with me.

She had such specific loves: cats, Spongebob, Elvis, and us, her family. Despite struggling with wanting Mom's acceptance, she never fully compromised herself. I remember her telling the kids, "If I could go back, I'd just make sure you know that life's too short not to live the way you want. Eat what you like, be healthy, and listen to Elvis and Michael Jackson every day." Susan never let go of her 3-inch nails or her purple hair; never traded her style or identity for a "golden crown." Some called her a "wigger" because she embraced the black community's culture, but that didn't bother her. That's where she found acceptance, where no one cared about diets or perfection, and her lack of "book smarts" didn't matter.

Yes, she wanted Mom's acceptance—what daughter doesn't? Eventually, she found some peace. When she left an abusive relationship and returned home, Mom welcomed her back. And when she found love with a kind black man, our family gave them a beautiful wedding. Susan was always about love, acceptance, and being true to herself. In the end, she taught me more than she ever could have imagined.

Susan's story didn't end with her leaving the pageant world. It was the beginning of a lifelong journey of defying expectations and challenging norms. Our mom was unrelenting in her pursuit of perfection, but Susan pushed back, especially when it came to embracing her own version of beauty and success. Her friends were like her—bold, unique, and often misunderstood by mainstream standards. They were artists, musicians, and kids who didn't fit into the carefully curated mold our mother wanted for us. Susan became a magnet for people who saw the world differently, and they were like a second family to her.

In a household that prized appearances, Susan's unapologetic authenticity was like a rebellious spark that couldn't be contained. She was the girl who would wear combat boots with her prom dress, and the one who'd sing her heart out to Michael Jackson in the middle of the grocery store, earning disapproving glances from strangers. I think part of her was fueled by a desire to show Mom—and everyone else—that there was no single way to be worthy, lovable, or beautiful.

One memory I hold close is from when I was around ten, and Susan decided to teach me how to dance. She had the living room stereo blasting Michael Jackson and Elvis Presley, two artists she adored. I remember her laughing as she tried to show me some moves, her purple hair bouncing as she spun around. She didn't just teach me to dance— she taught me to ignore what people thought and have fun in the moment. I remember her telling me, "Dancing isn't about how you look; it's about how you feel. Don't let anyone make you feel small because you're different."

When I got older, I learned about her first love, a man who brought her both joy and heartbreak. He was also her introduction to the struggles of loving someone from a different race in a family and society that often disapproved. Their relationship wasn't easy; they faced preju

dice and challenges from the outside and inside our family.

2017 with Mom and Poochie, then John, my son, Uncle Chris, Aunt Eve and Susan, far right with bright purple hair. She was 55 in this picture.

Our mom's disapproval weighed heavily on her, but Susan never let go of him easily. They fought to be together for a long time, and even after they separated, it left a mark on her. She loved deeply and fiercely, and though it sometimes brought her pain, she told me it was worth every moment.

For all her rebellious spirit, Susan carried the weight of her conflicts with our parents. I'd sometimes see her sitting quietly, deep in thought, and I knew she was thinking about our mother's expectations. Despite the hurt she felt from their rejection, she wanted her acceptance. The truth was, she loved Mom and Dad deeply, but she couldn't sacrifice herself to be the person they wanted her to be. She wanted their love without having to give up her essence.

When she finally left home, she moved to a neighborhood that was far removed from the polished suburban life we'd known. There, Susan found a place where she could be herself without judgment. Her friends became her new family, and she thrived. She worked odd jobs, from waitressing to singing in small clubs, always with a crowd of supportive friends cheering her on. She still called me often, reminding me to stay true to myself. I think she wanted me to learn from her battles, to see that it was possible to live a fulfilling life on one's own terms.

Years later, after her first marriage ended, Susan returned

to our family home for a time. By then, I was a teenager and saw her in a new light. She was bruised from her relationship, both emotionally and physically, but she never lost her sense of humor or her warmth. Susan's resilience was a beacon of strength for me; she taught me that even in heartbreak, there was room for healing and self-discovery.

As she got older, she found love again, this time with a man who truly understood her. They were a perfect fit, each accepting the other's quirks and past. For once, our family welcomed him with open arms, and they supported Susan and her new life.

On her wedding day, she didn't wear a traditional gown. Instead, she chose a dress that was uniquely her—brightly colored with a hint of sparkle. I'll never forget the smile on her face; she looked radiant, proud of her journey, and finally at peace with who she was.

Her advice stayed with me over the years, especially as I became a mother myself. I think back to her words often, especially when raising my girls. "Don't ever let anyone tell you who you should be," she'd say. "Love who you want, live how you want, and don't worry about fitting into anyone else's box." Susan's memory remains woven into my life, a reminder that real beauty lies in authenticity and that happiness can only come from living in alignment with who you truly are.

Now, when I think about her, I remember the countless lessons she taught me. She was more than just a "black sheep," she was a trailblazer, unafraid to live with boldness, laughter, and love. She showed me that we all deserve acceptance—whether we find it in our family or create it with those who embrace us for who we are. Her spirit lives on in the love I give to my own children, in the freedom I grant them to be themselves, and in the family I've created that, in her honor, celebrates individuality. I am grateful for the sister who showed me what it means to break free and live without limits. Even though she is no longer with us my older sister Susan had a message to share and I refuse to allow her to remain Speechless any longer.

**Crystal "Phoenix" Behe** is a Personality Recovery Specialist dedicated to guiding individuals from midlife crises to transformative personal rebirth. With a signature program that empowers clients to rise like a phoenix from the ashes of past challenges, Crystal Behe combines empathy, expertise, and a deep understanding of personal growth to help others embrace a renewed sense of purpose, strength, and fulfillment. You can learn more about her with the links below. www.Riseofcrystalphoenix.com

https://www.linkedin.com/in/crystal-behe
https://youtube.com/@crystalphoenix8320?
si=tNHoDaz3oRuN87bz

# LAFAYA MITCHELL …
# POKED SPEECHLESS

After my last bad run, I left the poker tournament thinking, "Why does this game I LOVE, piss me off SO much?" My heart was racing, I was feeling strong emotions ranging from wanting to cry to extreme rage with a little confusion mixed in. I was clearly and actively in "Red Alert Brain" mode.

Poker is a super logical, theory-based game with volatile variance that sometimes rattles the most robotic players in the world. "Bad beats" are more common than good wins, and losing happens 85% of the time for the best players in the world.

What a hugely masochistic way to aggravate a highly emotional little black girl with a severe trauma-based, poverty ridden, lack-based history causing her to be triggered easily by dangerous situations!

My only saving grace is "The Lafaya Way," (based on 4-Steps) I stumbled into after being forced to write a book series connected to my working successfully with Autism Spectrum and other neurodiverse disorders for over 20 years (long story behind "being forced.")

I was gifted the ability to literally give a voice to the voiceless with "The Lafaya Way." If you read the story

I shared about "blue tunnel boy" in my 1st parenting book, "The Lafaya Way: A Fresh Approach to Parenting

Hypersensitive Children;" it's a little story about a 7-year-old non-verbal boy on the Autism Spectrum who became verbal after 6-months of our working together.

"The Lafaya Way" parenting book series is basically a walk with me on how to live life in closer alignment with your truest intentions toward yourself and others. You learn how to interact in a way that gets your needs met, even when you or your loved one experiences challenges with hypersensitivity. Basically, a guide on "life-ing" at a high level.

So, if life-ing at a higher level is what you'd like to do, please feel free to read on.

"Red Alert Brain" is as it sounds: Heightened state of arousal= Uptick in dopamine cortisol, and adrenaline levels= Crisis Mode. The "Will Rogers, We Have a Problem Here" emotional state.

Red Alert Brain is experienced by every human; however, for some people, the distance traveled to get to the "dark side" tends to be a short one. The short distance travelers tend to be who I call hypersensitive. There are many contributing factors to hypersensitivity including but not limited to chemical imbalances, sensory sensitivities, traumatic history, susceptible temperament traits, failure to fit in socially, emotional dysregulation, etc.

I once had a client, I'll call him AB15, who expressed to me that he would shut down when upset, because trying to get intelligent words out of his mouth when he was really upset, was equivalent to trying to take an encyclopedia full of words and summarize them in one sentence. He had so many thoughts at the same time in his head that he was rendered speechless, unable to convey in words what his heart felt by the sheer overwhelm of having a negatively activated active brain.

One of the most misleading things about Red Alert Brain is how it manifests differently in different people or even differently in the same person depending on the day. Two commonly known Red Alert Brain (crisis) modes include:

Fight mode: yelling, screaming, crying, throwing things, hitting things...

OR

Flight mode: silent, shut down, escape, run away, isolate, self-medicate...

*Take a minute to think about what your crisis mode looks like.

No matter how crisis mode displays itself, the emotions behind it are PAINFUL. Reacting to painful emotions can cause you to become "stuck" in your pain. Becoming responsive to the message the pain is sharing with you can lead you into pathways of problem-solving and healing.

Personally, I am a bit of a hybrid, which can be a very upsetting, lonely, and EXTREMELY misunderstood place. Individual triggers and intensity of response can vary greatly, my daily moods vary greatly, and I give a whole new meaning to the word HANGRY when I neglect to get my three squares in. In other words, I am a CRAZY lady. I have often been left feeling judged, embarrassed, and ashamed of my own behaviors, because of course being a therapist who teaches calming tools; I should know better.

However, this wise lady told me, "You only need to be one step ahead of someone else to lead them." Not being too many steps ahead also means that I am not so far away that I can't reach them. So, HAH!

**Introducing The Lafaya Way:**

Background: I spent the better part of my youth in severe emotional pain. I remember putting a knife to my stomach at 7 years old, thinking: "How would I need to stab myself to die without it hurting too much? Maybe I could take a bunch of my mom's pills? How many? What if I didn't die? They'd have to pump my stomach, and I would be in so much trouble when I got home.  What if I did die? Would I go to Hell because I killed myself?"

It hurt so much to be here. I just wanted all the pain to stop. I would have similar thoughts to these well into my 30s. Of course, a lot has happened since then to change me. I no longer feel my emotional pain in a way that makes me feel it would be easier not to be on this earth. Feeling misunderstood by many no longer feels like a curse; I'm happy to be different. I definitely love me some me, and I treat myself with the same acceptance, grace, and love I expect from those I choose to allow in my "inner circle."

I didn't know, as it was being molded and developed in me, but The Lafaya Way has given me a pathway from very dark places to a new place full of love, light, hope, purpose and happiness as a choice. Do I still have dark thoughts on occasion? Yes, I do. Do I know how to kick those bad boys to curb and make way for better thoughts and the feeling attached? Yes, I do!

**The Lafaya Way 4 Core Steps:**

Think of The Lafaya Way 4 Core like the ingredients to a cake. If you're missing an ingredient you end up with a flat, ugly, and/or flat-out nasty cake. On the other hand, when you put all of the ingredients together, you end up with something DELICIOUS.

The acronym I use to help recall the 4 Steps more quickly is:

F.U.R.R.
F- Find Your Calm
U- Understand the Real Truth
R- Respond in Alignment w/Your Truest Intentions
R- The 3 Rs: Recognize Small Step Improvements, Reinforce Improvements Highly, Re-cycle through the 4 Steps.

Step 1: Find Your Calm:

I COULD NOT STAND when people would tell me, "You just need to calm down," when I was having a clearly tough meltdown moment. I remember thinking, "Do you think I WANT to feel like this? If I could calm down, I WOULD!"

This is one of the BIG reasons behind my choosing *Find* your calm as my step one. What I've found is that it's not impossible to calm down; it's just REALLY hard depending on how far into crisis mode you are. Also, there must be a lifeline- something to grab ahold of so that you don't fall into the blackhole our emotions can become.

One of the common attacks on a sensitive person's system is having to be around or deal with negative energy coming from others. Hypersensitive people tend to be plagued by a phenomenon that I call "Emotion-Soaking." Emotion-Soaking is the unintentional sponging of the "feeling" energies of those around you. (example: picture of a flat sponge reflecting no negative emotion transfer and an enlarged sponge that has soaked in someone's negative energy transfer.)

Just living in this world full of drama-craving drones can be a nightmare for hypersensitive individuals. Getting out of bed can mean being instantly bombed by negative feelings pouring out of a cranky parent, sibling, or other loved one. We need a coat of armor or 'shields up' just to prevent ourselves from taking direct hits all day. No wonder our systems are all torn up and easily sent into red alerts.

What we put more energy into grows. Finding your calm is important to prevent and/or cool the effects of "Red Alert Brain." Our brain's default reaction to being triggered is fight/flight mode. We have the right to choose to override that system and go into the more calming problem-solving mode.

The two main keys to Finding Your Calm are:

1. Don't Personalize. (This concept is borrowed from Don Miguel Ruiz's book, "The Four Agreements".) Basically, taking someone else's issues, struggles, mistakes and making them about you instead of keeping their problems about them, this can be detrimental to our ability to be calm. It is impossible to feel offended, disrespected, and/ or mistreated and peaceful and calm at the same time. However, when you are able to make the shift to feeling empathic towards another human being that is acting in a way that will get less of their needs met, then you are pointing yourself towards the pathway to peace.

For example: Someone is not feeling heard or understood, so they yell; yelling only likely causes a shut down or yell back reaction, completely working against their goal to feel heard and understood. If you can see their yelling as a lack of communication skills that works against them, you will not feel personally offended by their yelling.

Is thinking in this way VERY difficult to do, especially in a heated moment? Hell YES! However, it is not impossible and gets easier with practice. I mean, did LeBron James pick up the basketball the 1$^{st}$ time and have amazing handles? No. He practiced his butt off until he was the best; then when he was the best, he still kept practicing, keeping his edge.

2. Monitor and Balance your Physical Cues to Upset. Some physical cues to upset include: pounding/racing heart, shallow breathing, tensing muscles, heating up (feeling extra hot.) These physical cues send a message to the brain that the body is in danger and in need of protection, which then kicks flight/fight into gear. It's an ancient protective mechanism built into the brain for survival (i.e.: see dinosaurs, hide, run, fight or die!)

With no impending doom, it is important to slow down the red alert effects that happen in the brain and body by first thinking, "Ok, no dinosaurs chasing me, so this racing heart, shallow breathing, etc., is just telling me there was something that happened that I didn't like very much." Time to counter the cues to upset. First things first: take a deep breath (inhale 5-count, exhale 6-count or pick a deep breathing technique you like.) Deep breathing counters shallow breathing, gets more oxygen to the brain to improve your ability to think and helps to slow down that speedy heart rate; it's a three-fer.) Another physical cue balancing action is to relax your muscles: un-ball those fists, relax those shoulder muscles or wherever you're holding your tension, make your whole body go limp like a ragdoll. The "ragdoll" technique is for when you are alone and preferably sitting or lying down; looks weird if you just melt into the floor in front of someone else. If you're hot, dampen a towel with cold water and rub it against your skin. If it is causing your cues to go crazy to be in a certain environment or around a certain person, take a walk to cool off.

Basically, countering the cues to upset is exactly as it sounds. DO something non-harmful to yourself or others to battle the flood of physical cues that show up when you're being triggered towards crisis mode.

The two keys mentioned above can go a long way in helping you find your Calm. You can find more in-depth conversation on all the steps in "The Lafaya Way" book series.

Step 2: Understand the "REAL" Truth

As mentioned above, the 4 Core steps work together like the ingredients in a cake. Understanding the real truth is also a great way to assist with finding your Calm. Getting to the REAL truth is often not as simple as it sounds though. There are many 'think they're truths' we tell ourselves that are more based in perception (which varies for everyone) than they are in the real truth.

It can be VERY tough to get to the "real" truth. Two Keys:

1. Use helpful check-in acronyms such as H.A.L.T. (from

12-steps program) and J.I.M. (A Lafaya Way original) to identify potential truths behind your own and others' reactions.

**H**ungry  **J**udgment
**A**ngry  **I**nvalidation
**L**onely  **M**isunderstanding
**T**ired

2. Put yourself in a truly empathetic space by asking yourself questions that cause you to take a deeper look into the actions/reactions of others.

a. **What might be hurting them?** Ask this question without judging how they feel or comparing those feelings to others'.

b. **What benefit might they be trying to get from their words/actions?** Ask yourself this question, and consider that it harms them more and keeps them from getting their needs met when their reasons appear to be manipulative. Perceived manipulation tends to cause upset and creates an atmosphere where they do not get their needs met. Adjust your perception to see manipulation as self-harm, and to prevent yourself from becoming indignant towards, or feeling disrespected by, the identified manipulator.

c. **If I were them, how would I want to be taught to adapt/adjust?** Would you want someone yelling at you or being angry with you as they taught you, or would you want them to be more loving and helpful? Once you have your answer, respond accordingly.

Understanding the "real" truth requires that you ask yourself the questions that allow you to acquire deeper insight into your own and other's experiences.

*For particularly annoying people that seem to get extremely reinforced by your negative reactions "emotional stimming" might be at play.

Emotional Stimming is seeking after strong sensory input by way of evoking strong internal emotional reactions from others. This type of stimming is very self-sabotaging for those that engage in it.

** Please keep in mind that all humans NEED to feel connected, loved, and understood. If anyone appears as if they don't need or care about these things, an injury has occurred at some point that surely causes them a great deal of pain.

Step 3: Respond in Alignment w/Your Truest Intentions

I remember a time when I used to "play myself" all the time. I'd pridefully fight against my own desires, oblivious to the fact that I was actually more responsible for not getting my needs met than the person I was blaming for not meeting my needs.

I thought bashing the other people that I strongly desired to feel close to would snap them to their senses and they'd see how important it was to do what I wanted them to do. Then I'd be deeply hurt by their negative reaction to my attempt to strong-arm my needs out of them.

My methods were to say the least COMPLETELY ineffective and often achieved the exact opposite of what I REALLY wanted. I wanted closeness but pushed them further away with my poor choice of judgmental, anger-filled words. I'd want peace, but would yell, scream, and stomp about like a tampering toddler. I'd desire to feel loved but spewed hateful words. I had no idea how important it was to respond in alignment with my truest desires.

You must have a recognized target to hit said target. You can't just put "somewhere" in your GPS and expect that it'll take you to the location you would like to get to. In life, if you are not clear on or keep your gaze on your core goals, you often can't stay true to being intentional about getting what you want.

### 2 keys to responding in alignment with your own truest intentions:

1. Ask yourself, what are my core goals in life?

At the deepest level, most humans desire to have a life filled with peace, love, happiness, and connection through community (everybody does their part.)

Other more actualized individuals may also include empowerment through personal growth and ability to live in alignment with their life's purpose.

***Stop for a moment and list 3 Core Goals that you have for your life.

2. Empowerment Talk Formula:

I understand that you…(insert the tough experience s/he may be having), but
When you…                  (upsetting behavior)
It causes…                  (undesired reaction)

And I know that is not your intention,
So please…                  (more acceptable response)

## Empowerment Talk Formula in Action:

You're clearly upset about me staying out too late yesterday, but

When you yell at me, it causes me to get defensive more than hear you

And I know that is not your intention

So please try to talk to me without yelling, so I can try to respond the way you need me to.

The Empowerment Talk Formula gives you a validating and non-judgmental way to communicate in tough situations. It helps to decrease defensiveness and promotes working together to get everyone's needs better met.

Step 4: 3-Rs= Recognize, Reinforce, Repeat

Step 4 is my Growth-Minded Step. It brings light and hope to tough situations by focusing on small step improvements as opposed to the problems that still exist. This step is good at battling perfectionism and 'all or nothing' thinking.

### 3-R Breakdown

**Recognize**- Recognize the "small step" wins; this increases your faith in the possibility of positive change. Make a consistent effort to acknowledge when there's been progress; the alternative is to expect overall/perfection/ huge leap changes and constantly feel disappointed that you are not reaching your goal.

**Reinforce**- Highly reinforce the positive changes that you see (in both you and others.) Reinforcement serves to:

- Build self-esteem (a yes, we can do this spirit)

- Put more energy into the things we want more of
- Keep us properly balanced (evens us out, so that we're not considered mostly a complainer)

- instinctually humans tend to be highly reactive to those things that are perceived as "danger," it's our survival instinct (see dinosaur must avoid the danger.) Translate the danger experience to relationships: the other person is doing something to "make" you "feel" not so good, so you must "do" something about that

-we are not instinctually reactive to those things that are the "safe" things (i.e., expected/desired behaviors from others.) Often, when we get "desired" behaviors from others, it does not elicit a strong (survival instinct-type) response from us, so it can often unintentionally go ignored.

**For example:** Step 4ing it in poker means recognizing that my being pissed off about taking a bad beat looks VERY DIFFERENT now than it did not that long ago. I've gone from full on meltdowns which included cussing out the other players involved in the hand, the dealer, and anybody else who had the nerve to make a comment; to holding it in at the table and then scream-crying while punching the roof of my car  all the way home; to speeding dangerously fast on the freeway, verbally unleashing my anger out on 'bad drivers;' to NOW yelling "FUCK" a couple of times in the car and turning my favorite song way up and singing all the bad energy out. Those incremental small step improvements are worth acknowledging and patting myself on the back for. Acknowledging my improvements keeps me from judging myself for getting upset when I should 'know better than being upset about a game' and gives me hope that I'll be able to one day display the classy demeanor of respected world champions.

**Repeat-** Stay aware of the importance of constantly flowing through (working) the Core 4 Steps. It's how to relate to others in a healthy and productive way.

*I owe it to these methods for a calmer life and
an ever-improving poker game.*

Summing It All Up

I got to learn a HUGE life lesson by accidentally burning my leg on the grill of a motorcycle. Oh, it burned me so good that it gave me the opportunity to see healing from the inside out, live and in-person. I watched the burnt portion of my lower leg, with all the skin missing, heal slowly and painfully. No matter how much I wished to have skin back in that spot, it was not going to happen until all the necessary inner healing took place.

It hit me that physical and emotional healing are one in the same. The deeper the wound, the more time it takes to heal; it takes an even longer time to re-develop a layer of protection against infection. When the skin (protective covering) finally grew back, it brought with it what I originally experienced as ugly scarring. The scar was a forever reminder of my stupid mistake.

The memory of emotional trauma never truly leaves our body, but we can make a choice to use that knowledge in our favor. You can lament, regret, and hate the scar, which causes continued emotional pain OR you can proudly display the scar, and use it as a beautiful defining characteristic of who you are NOW.

I must admit that I defaulted to lamenting and hating my physical and emotional scars for many years, but today I choose to use them to change lives for the better.

I'm calling you out to work towards doing the same for yourself. Create some room in your life for your newly introduced F.U.R.R. friends. Embrace the idea of knowing what buttons to push to give yourself and others the opportunity to speak from your real truth freely and powerfully. Finding Your Calm, Understanding the Real Truth, Responding in Alignment with Your Truest Intentions, Recognizing and Reinforcing the Small Step Improvements in Yourself and Others, will usher in a new way of life-ing that makes the people you deal with (including yourself) feel heard, validated and valued. I eluded a new favorite quote of mine earlier:

**"My mouth can't translate the things my
heart says"- (unknown author)**

It is my hope that we all become better expressers of our Truest Desires and that "Red Alert Brain" no longer holds our voices captive.

**Lafaya Mitchell**, Licensed Marriage and Family Therapist, wife, and reluctant, but happy mother of six is on a mission to calm the effects of those experiencing "Red Alert Brain." She aspires to share her life changing philosophy, "The Lafaya Way" (created in over 20 years of real life and professional experience) with the world.

She has published three books in "The Lafaya Way" parenting series, and has created a 12-week curriculum that creates pathways to healthy and effective interactions with hypersensitive children.

Since "The Lafaya Way" is essentially the pathway to fostering living life in alignment with your truest intentions, Lafaya has also found a way to apply her 4-step methodology to other situations such as battling T.I.L.T. in Poker (a tough sport she has learned to LOVE over the past 15 years).

Ms. Mitchell offers support by way of individual, and family counseling. She also provides training, and consultation to schools and other community-based organizations.

**Social Media Links:**

Instagram: instagram.com/lafaya_way
  or instagram.com/lafayawaypoker

Websites:  lafayaway.com and lafayawaypoker.com

# SABRINA SCHOTTENHAMEL ... ENCOURAGING AN INTROVERT'S HEART IN AN EXTROVERTED WORLD

"Hey Dawn! Are you ready for the party? I'm super excited to meet some new people!"

"Oh, well, that's, um, Anna, uhm, it's actually why I'm calling…"

She barely squeaked out the words, her voice quivering the whole time. The growing lump in her throat made it even harder for her to speak.

"Yeah, I'm just not, umm, feeling good. I have to stay home. Ya know, don't wanna get anyone else sick."

"What!? NO! You can't cancel last minute! Ughhhh!" Anna was angry and quickly hung up.

I know how it feels, my dear fellow introvert. Guess what? It doesn't have to be that way forever.

Have you ever felt so strongly that you wanted to be an extrovert? Think about this, though: how can you fit into a mold that doesn't allow you to climb into it?

Extroverts seem to have it easy, as if life rolls so smoothly for them. Conversely, we introverts have a different shape that doesn't roll quite so smoothly: we are more of a heart shape in a circular world. The heart is the stem to our internal thoughts. We stand on the point and waiver with the wind of the extroverts.

~

Did you know?
"Shyness" and being an introvert are not the same. Shyness comes when you're unsure of what to expect or feel less than in a group of possibly more wise people. Even extroverts can feel shy at times.

~

I call myself 'a developing extrovert.' As the leader of a small networking group for introverts, I know how to nurture and guide my fellow introverts to move past social hurdles like Dawn's. I was once there, too. What I found, and what the group members consistently tell me, is how the group environment helps introverts, like us, open up in a supportive and safe way.

We are not trying to be someone else because God made us all special and unique, so remember to celebrate who, and how, you are. Instead of feeling alone or left out, shift your thinking into learning something new. Keep sharp! We can observe skills from the extroverts around us in order to be able to step into that role, at times. Yes, we can all learn new skills as a developing extrovert. Doing so will give you a bigger zone of comfort, learning and experiences. Remember to remain as you are... you are quiet yet powerful, so stand in your power as you develop new skills to grow into your life's purpose.

I want you to feel comfortable when speaking up to your extroverted counterparts. This creates and ensures better relationships, overall.

Gulp! Does this topic generate some apprehension? That's perfectly normal. I am here to assure you that it takes a bit of courage in the beginning but with guidance and practice it can be accomplished (in your favor.)

Three steps to speak up and ask for what you want or need.
- Breathe in confidence
- Stand strong in your worth
- Have accountability

What do I mean by 'breathe in confidence'? Before you speak up, take time to center yourself by breathing. Practice some self-care techniques that boost your energy and confidence. Once you are prepared, you can have a conversation from a place of truth and love. The other person will feel your ((heart)), and in turn, be more open to listening.

'Stand strong in your worth' means believing that what you have to say is important. The world is a little sweeter when we, as introverts, speak up and share our gifts to enhance others.

Finding a group to have your back at any time will assure a stronger sense of 'supportability.' (Supportability: finding 'your' group that will support you with your needs with love and accountability.)

The root of my introverted behavior began in first grade, and the impact lasted far too long. The crazy thing is I took on a label and realized I was wearing a lie.

I was held back in first grade.

For so many years I wore a label that said, "I am stupid" because of it. Being held back gave me a complex that I wasn't good enough, smart enough or had what it took to keep up with my classmates. I put that label on myself. Nobody ever called me stupid - I did that all on my own. Isn't it funny how we can do that to ourselves? Have you ever labeled yourself? Well, maybe it's time to peel off that label for good! All it did was cause me to pull in, hide and stop asking questions.

At the same time, my spirit loved to shine through the art of dance. I performed my heart out in front of hundreds of people because it felt safe. It was the only way I was able to express myself. I was naturally talented in dance, ballet, in particular. Moving my body gave me genuine confidence - that it was OK to have an expression of self. That was the only time I didn't want to change who I was because in those moments, I was comfortable in the spotlight.

I realize now how the struggle of speaking up has become a gift. I had silenced myself in the past and lived as a shy and anxious introvert. But because of those experiences, I can relate to feeling less than.

Then, one day I decided I wanted more. Toastmasters and public speaking were on my radar. For over a year I fought in silence about attending a Toastmasters meeting. Once I finally mustered up the courage to attend, a spark was lit inside. That was in April of 2013. That spark led me to speak actively at the meetings and in 2015, I won the Best Speaker of the Year award! This major boost in confidence changed only everything for me.

As you're reading this you may be thinking, "Wow, it

Sabrina Schottenhamel
The Introverted Speaker

seemed so easy for her." Let me tell you, it wasn't. It was a lot of struggles - internal and external. Crafting a speech, practicing it and then delivering it takes a chunk of time and effort. Literally blood, sweat and tears. Our minds play tricks on us in the process when we are trying to develop ourselves into a better person. It tells us lies like, "You're not good enough" or "Who do you think you are?" In those many moments, I wanted to quit. But there's always been another, louder voice telling me, 'Go for it, Sabrina!' Let me tell you, all that time of sticking to it has opened the doors of confidence to keep going, put myself out there, be criticized and yet earn respect from others.

Since then, I have stepped away from Toastmasters to pursue growing my network as a professional speaker. My experience will always stick with me and carry me forward. Yes, I have days where I don't feel like things are going my way... but those are the days I find my community and reach out to ask for help.

Another BIG key has been to keep persevering through the tough times, over and over. Asking myself many times, "Am I still on the right path?"

**As Zig Ziglar said, "Getting knocked down in life is a given. Getting up and moving forward is a choice."**

When we get knocked down we must pick ourselves up and overcome. Since I am a developing extrovert, some days I feel like I am on top of the world yet other days, I want to continue to hide in the shadows because it's safe. Hiding doesn't allow us to overcome anything, so we must get out there and be vulnerable. Another reason why we need community. As human beings, we are *all* meant for community, so find yours and cherish it.

When I began as a Toastmaster, I found this kind of community. I didn't realize it at first, but it was a safe place for me to practice my speeches before going out into the professional world. My fellow Toastmasters were a group that supported me and gave constructive and positive feedback so that I could improve and be encouraged to continue striving to become better, all because I found my group.

<blockquote>"Nothing worth having comes easy." - Theodore Roosevelt</blockquote>

I love speaking to emerging leaders because the moment the message hits their hearts their eyes light up.

This has not been a simple walk in the park, in fact every time I am scheduled to speak I tell myself I am excited but deep down I hope the event will cancel or some crazy storm will occur causing me to be stuck - stuck in the comfort of my own home. That's where I feel most safe. If that did happen every time, I'd still be the same person, without growth, challenges or perseverance.

Have you ever felt like you'd rather have a natural disaster happen than do something scary? I believe a lot of us have been there. You're not alone, you are a developing extrovert.

Back to the main point of when fear sets in... The big day arrives and I'm finally up on stage speaking and I remember how much I love it. What an incredible feeling it is to share the knowledge, wisdom and experiences with my audience. Being up on stage now has full circle moments because it reminds me of my days of dancing my heart out as a young girl.

Over time I have realized I'm able to shine my light the brightest when all my activities revolve around the theme of creativity and art. What lights you up?

I've finally created an organized guide for introverts to give them the confidence they're looking for in preparation for social events. "Networking As An Introvert Framework" is the passion project I've been developing since 2021. It's a set, yet flexible framework of what activities to schedule before, during and after social events. There's even a supporting guide of Icebreaker Questions and Topics you can study before going out in social or professional environments. That way you will have quality questions, top-of-mind, to keep conversations going without that awkward silence. Be sure to take advantage of these free resources so that you can go out into the world with a pep in your step! Remember, you are not alone.

*Pause and reflect for a few moments on these:*
Where in life were you held back?
Did you hold yourself back or did someone else?
Where in life do you see God trying to reveal your gifts to you?
Do you have a common theme that keeps showing up for

you in your life?

You reading this chapter is not an accident. Ask yourself, "Is it time for a change?" If the answer is a BIG 'Yes!' You may have a developing extrovert that's wanting to come out too.

Please use my linktree, below, and check out my free resources. Be sure to register for our monthly NFI (Networking for Introverts) group calls. It is in this small group setting where we can go deeper into these topics. I promise you will be filled with love, encouragement and feel at ease to be yourself with us there.

Please reach out to me! I'm looking forward to being your cheerleader.

"Now, I know I am worthy of God's love by learning about the gifts He has given me."
~ with Love,
Sabrina Schottenhamel

Thank you for sharing my chapter with others you know who struggle to speak up.

**Sabrina Schottenhamel** is on a mission to empower introverts to use their voice, speak up and shine, not hide.

Speaking was a challenge when Sabrina was a child but on the other hand could dance and perform her heart out in front of hundreds.

Becoming an entrepreneur pushed Sabrina to grow professionally. In 2013 she joined Toastmasters and that led her to overcome her fears of public speaking. Shortly thereafter, Sabrina won the 2015 Best Speaker of the Year

Award!!

Since then Sabrina has stepped into the professional speaking space. All of this experience has led her to speak & educate all around empowering introverts.

In 2021, Sabrina started an intimate group called, Networking for Introverts. Since then the overall feedback from the attendees is that it's a safe space to learn, open up and share ideas together without judgment.

Find Sabrina on LinkedIn and for more free resources go to https://linktr.ee/Sabrinaschottenhamel

# ALECIA C. TOLVER ... HONOR YOUR MOTHER

"Honor your father and mother, that your days may long upon the land which the Lord your God is giving you." – Exodus 20:12 NKJV

Can love and hate coexist in the same heart? It's a confusing feeling—loving someone so deeply that life feels incomplete without them yet feeling an intense frustration that makes you question why you care at all. My mother has a remarkable ability to evoke this duality in me more often than I'd like to admit.

I vividly remember a painful moment after my second miscarriage. I was on the phone with her, grappling with my sadness. I hadn't shared this news with many people, but I felt it was important for her to know. The first time I miscarried, she comforted me with a simple, "Ah suh ih guh sometimes, it's alright, God knows best." But this time, her words stung: "Ah wah yuh duh mek yuh ah lose baby suh?"— "What is wrong with you that you keep losing babies?"

In that moment, I was taken aback. Did she really think it was my fault? Anger surged through me like a tidal wave. I wanted to unleash my feelings, to express how hurtful her response was, but instead, I found myself silent—just saying "uhhmm" and listening like a timid child. When she finally paused, I knew I had to go. I hung up the phone feeling disappointed and frustrated—not just with her words but with my own inability to speak up. I've always tried to honor my mother and avoid disrespecting her, but sometimes it feels impossible. In that moment of vulnerability, she missed the mark completely; she didn't provide the comfort I desperately needed. It was as if she didn't even try to understand my pain.

"I can do all things through Christ who strengthens me." – Philippians 4:13 (NIV)

Yet, God has a way of teaching us lessons through our experiences. Reflecting on that day, I realized that many women endure miscarriages without even knowing they were pregnant. The emotional weight of loss can be heavy, especially when you're already battling self-blame. Despite that painful conversation, my mother has been there for me in countless ways throughout my life. After my children were born, her support was invaluable—even when it sometimes felt overwhelming. She wanted to help so much that it often left me feeling incapable of managing on my own terms. Don't get me wrong; I love my mother dearly. Her presence during those early months of motherhood—alongside the support of my husband—was a lifeline for me. She has shown up for me in ways that have saved my life. But when it comes to navigating complex emotions, she struggles.

Growing up in Jamaica shaped her perspective—a culture where honesty often trumps empathy. In a world where survival takes precedence over emotional expression, many mothers had to grow up fast and adapt quickly.

Meet Moummy Cinderella—my mother's affectionate name for herself. Not the fairy tale kind of Cinderella waiting for rescue but a hardworking woman who cooked and cared for her siblings from an early age. She migrated to the United States in her late 20s with three children in tow, carrying with her the traditions and values of her upbringing. As we settled into this new land filled with uncertainty, I often felt lost—like a stranger in a foreign world without any relatable stories or experiences to guide me. Yet through it all, Moummy remained a constant presence in my life.

Isn't it remarkable how some people shape our lives without us realizing their impact until they're no longer there? My mother—a blend of "Mommy" and "Mum"—is one such gift.

There's something profound about how our relationships evolve over time. As I navigate motherhood myself, I see reflections of both my mother and myself in my children's behaviors—often those traits I wish to improve upon most.

My mother wasn't as voiceless as she may have thought. Her message was making its way through. Her wisdom resonates deeply within me as I navigate the challenges of my own life. She taught me the importance of taking time for myself amidst life's chaos. "You only have one life fi live; don't let bills stop you from enjoying it." Her encouragement inspires me to embrace life fully, taking vacations and pursuing what brings me joy rather than merely existing for work or obligations.

Her lessons about living fully resonate deeply within me, shaping not only my perspective but also my approach to motherhood. She's taught me that life is too precious to be spent solely on responsibilities; it's essential to carve out moments for joy and connection. Her words echo in my mind as I navigate the beautiful disorder of raising my own children: "Yuh betta live yuh life." My babies have become the center of my world, igniting a fierce desire to be the best version of myself. They are my motivation, my inspiration, and my greatest teachers. Every day, as I look into their curious eyes, I'm reminded of the profound impact I have on their lives. I want to make positive changes and affect their lives in the best way possible, breaking cycles and creating new, healthier patterns.

This desire to be better for my children often brings me back to reflect on my relationship with my own mother. While we've had our struggles and misunderstandings, her strength and resilience have undeniably shaped who I am today. I find myself drawing on her wisdom, even as I strive to forge my own path in motherhood.

There's a beautiful complexity in this generational connection. As I work to provide my children with the emotional support and understanding I sometimes felt was missing in my own upbringing, I also recognize the invaluable lessons my mother imparted. Her emphasis on enjoying life amidst responsibilities now takes on new meaning as I balance the demands of motherhood with the need for self-care and joy.

"The days are long, but the years are short." – Gretchen Rubin

My babies make me acutely aware of the passage of time and the importance of creating meaningful memories. I want to show them a mother who is present, who laughs often, who takes time for herself, and who pursues her passions. In doing so, I hope to honor my mother's teachings while also addressing the emotional needs that I've come to recognize as crucial. As I navigate this journey, I'm learning that perfection isn't the goal. Like my mother,

I'm doing the best I can with what I have. Her words remind me that while we may not always have everything figured out, we can find comfort in each other's presence.

This sentiment now extends to the bond I'm nurturing with my own children. In the end, my babies have become the bridge between generations – a living reminder of where I've come from and a promise of where I'm going. They inspire me to heal, to grow, and to love more deeply than I ever thought possible. Through them, I'm learning to embrace both the joys and challenges of motherhood, creating a legacy of love, understanding, and resilience that I hope will echo through generations to come.

Through all of this, I hope that my mother understands how deeply she is loved—not just by me, but by God as well. This is a vital message and reminder that I hold close to my heart: we are all worthy. We were created with intention and purpose, and it is our responsibility to discover and define what that purpose is. Her purpose goes far beyond raising five children and working hard to create the best environment possible under the circumstances of life's journey. She showed up every day ready to give a little bit more than she received and her strength and resilience have shaped who I am today, allowing me to adapt and overcome obstacles with grace and determination. The relationship between a mother and child is beautifully complex – a spectrum of experiences where some days are easier than others. There is no perfect way; there is only what works for us as we journey through life together.

We may not always get it right or provide each other with exactly what we need every moment, but with love, there is a space for grace, kindness, and compassion even when words fail us. In the end, we do our best with what we have

– and that is enough.

Reflecting on our relationship, I realize how much I appreciate my mother's unwavering support, even when it sometimes feels overwhelming. She has shown up for me in countless ways, especially during the early months of motherhood when I needed it the most. Her presence was a helping hand I didn't know I needed, helping me to navigate the challenges of caring for my little ones.

Yet, I also recognize that expressing emotions can be difficult for both of us. There have been moments when I've longed for comfort and understanding, but instead felt a disconnect. It's in those times that I wish we could communicate more openly about our feelings – sharing both our joys and our struggles without fear of misunderstanding.

Moummy Cinderella is a remarkable woman, molded by her experiences in Jamaica and the challenges of life in a new country. Her honesty and practicality have shaped my perspective on many things including how I approach my own motherhood. I see reflections of me in my children's behaviors – both the traits I admire and those I strive to improve upon.

"Give thanks to the Lord, for he is good. His love endures." – Psalms 136:1 (NIV)

Dear reader, never forget that you are deeply loved and valued. Your journey has touched countless lives in ways that words alone cannot express. As we navigate the unique dynamics of our relationships, let us commit to communicating openly and supporting one another through life's ups and downs. Embrace those you love, allowing them to fulfill their purpose in your life, and cherish the gifts they bring for your own growth and self-discovery. Remember, it is through these connections that we find strength, healing, and the courage to become our best selves. In the end, love is the most powerful force we have—it can transform pain into purpose and turn struggles into strength.

"Love and hate - can never be friends." - Dennis Brown (Jamaican singer)

**A.C. Tolver**, Jamaican born American raised transformation agent, U.S. Army Veteran, coach, mentor, growing woman of God, wife and mother. On a mission to change the world and be the change that she wants to see in it. She is an aspiring motivational speaker who speaks on the dynamics of leadership and honing your ability to serve others through self-leadership and continuous growth. She has traveled to multiple countries and had countless cultural experiences that have sowed the seeds of curiosity and love for the beauty that the world has to offer. She wants to share her experiences and stories with others to influence and encourage a shift for the better. She believes that you should never lose who you are but enhance who you are destined to become.

# LONNEE REY ... THE LIGHT
# IN OUR LIVES

*"When I stand before God at the end of my life, I would hope that I would not have a single bit of talent left, and could say, 'I used everything you gave me."— Erma Bombeck*

On October 14th, I got a message from my dear friend Michelle Laaks. She was concerned about the hurricane that hit Tennessee. She was always so considerate and concerned. However, that message also contained something that concerned me: "Have a deep share, need to talk." The phone call that followed was like being hit with a wrecking ball: "I got the results. You're the first person I've spoken to about it. It's fourth stage cancer." (deep breath) I jumped into solution-mode, suggesting Essiac tea. She agreed to order it right away. We discussed what to do next. I was going to help her write a foreword for Emily's book, and maybe her full story, to keep her mind occupied, but I never heard from her again…

Few knew how she'd suffered all year long, enduring extreme pain, not knowing what was wrong with her, waiting months to see a doctor, only to be less-informed than ever after each visit. She was pretty good about hiding how bad she felt until finally, she simply could not do it any longer. The can-do gal in everyone's life took a rest on the sidelines of life, hoping, as always, to get back in the game.

Most people don't know this, but we discussed my moving to South Africa. She even said she would marry me just to keep me there, safe and sound, out of the US for so many reasons. I never imagined the day that it would not be an option.

On October 26th, I got a message from her long-time friend and housemate, Amanda: *"Sadly yet with relief Michelle is now at peace."* OH noooo. Not yet! NO. No way! How could this be true? She wasn't done, yet. A cold wind rustled through a hole in the fabric of the Universe - and a star just went dark.

On Nov 2, 2024, a celebration of her life was attended by 20 or more of us on Zoom and over 100 people on the property where she lived in South Africa. The show of love all along the way to this day was incredible. I jokingly called her 'Sister Mary Sunshine.' Apparently, I wasn't the only person who basked in her radiance.

Amanda: "The Way"

The way you touched our world.
the way you were your authentic self.
the way you spoke your truth.
you're crazy creative passions.
this all created a ripple effect on everyone.
the way you loved all animals.
the way you laughed out loud.
the way you always gave freely.
the way you loved.
this all created a ripple effect on everyone.

~

She went through a lot after discovering her family of origin and the stories behind her adoption. I got to meet her when she was ready to make something of it …
Michelle was hell-bent on making sure that others shared their story and their legacy message before it was too late.

We did a couple of books together in the "Rattled Awake" series. Sharing her adoption story and encouraging others to find their adoptive families, (because it brought her *so* much happiness), was her message. She wanted others to have closure, or an opening, but something so they didn't die wondering…so they would pass with "NO Regrets" (the name of her chapter in "Rattled Awake: Volume Five.")

Chiyedza Nyahue, a "Rattled Awake: Volume Three" co-author with Michelle, said it perfectly in her review:

"Michelle, your story is a powerful reminder,

*"Don't let the music die with you." - Wayne Dyer*

Oh how we know so well those inner gifts that we tend to tuck away as we are schooled by certain biases that we can't make a living from. So we hide them away, focusing on building a "career" that keeps a roof over our heads. What a beautiful, loving gift your mother refocused for you. Your Art with heArt taps into your divine purpose to use your art as an instrument of healing, showing people how radiant, uniquely beautiful we are individually and as collective humanity. Your courageous reclamation of your divine given talents, that intimate human touch that no technology can replicate, definitely breaks and stomps on confined boxes. The illustrations included in your story does make one take a pause to give yourself permission to experience and even inspire what can be, by pushing the boundaries of creative expression, with childlike freedom. We celebrate you Mich as you bravely bring your phenomenal talent to illuminate our world!"

I asked Michelle's friends & family to give me a few lines to commemorate what Michelle left behind for them:

>From her sister, Tamra: A true inspiration in never leaving an area unmarked in her encouragement In her passions. an animal healer and an artist that gives everyone a color of her spirit... the brightest colors of a picture perfect sister.

>Mel: A sister to love, respect and true memories to never forget. I love you till we meet again to hug. Love, Mel.

>Licia: Fast! it all happened so fast, and it feels like your time with us was too short. But then pause, take a breath, and see all the lives you touched, the people you connected with, and remember how at peace you were.. Deep breath ... Left in silence and lost for words... Michelle, you will be missed and never forgotten. With love, Licia.

>Cheryl Bennett: She gave up a high-powered job to pursue her passions and talents...to live a life of uncertainty. She had the courage to take that step of faith, to pursue her dreams. She sacrificed a lot but there was no going back.

And if someone needed her, she dropped everything to be there. For me, that meant 2hr drives each way for weeks; it meant taking care of me when no one else could; it meant sacrificing her passion to help people for as long as it took.

~

I used to flip her shit for working more shifts. Her back was really hurting, and it was time she stopped being a hero. She prided herself on being stubborn, and so, off to work she went. The people she worked with adored Michelle. Anke, owner of the food truck where Mich busted-butt on weekends,

working hard
hardly working - same-same

sent a message from the team: "A continuous positive happy attitude and always positive encouragement - she made everyone's day!"

Her buoyant and bubbly nature could lift Eyeore out of the doldrums, I swear.

>Big Baba Little Baba sent this: I would like to say how positive Mich was to life - (no matter what happened) she made a plan (for the future.) The LOVE she projected was out of this world. Her legacy (family) meant the world to her. She taught me love, understanding, patience, peace like no other. Her animals were her solitude. Everything about her was for the better good of life.

~

"*What* are you doing?!" I said.

"OH, I've got this baby chic on my lap, wrapped in a heating pad, hoping he lives. He's pretty near being a flattie, though." She laughed.

"That's not funny, Michelle," I didn't know what a flattie was but it didn't sound good.

"It is, Lonnee! You should see this!" (long pause) "Oh well… now he's a flattie." She roared with laughter. "He didn't make it." More laughter. "You should see them when they die - it's why we call them flatties - they get all deflated!" More laughter.

I loved her laugh. The giggles about 'tragedy' lightened the mood.

She inspired me to match her brevity. "Hey, what do you think about doing a story in my next book, *Fur Baby Confessions*? We can call it, *My Life with Chicks*." Hilarious, given her love of women, but she laughingly declined.

"I'd love to, but I just don't feel that good, Lonnee."

◆ ◆ ◆

>From Lisa Marree: Jim Rohn said,
*"Life is brief, even at its longest."*

My belief is nothing happens by accident on life's timeline.

I was blessed to have my own brief moments with Michelle over the past 12 months, such an incredible soul with so much joy and love in her heart for humans and animals. Our friendship led to a number of very powerful connections, again, not by accident, including my dear friend and Editor in Chief of this book, plus multiple other 'Best Sellers', Lonnee Rey.

Michelle was not only able to turn her powerful life story of her discovery of adoption into purpose and impact in recent anthologies such as "Rattled Awake" series, but also leave her talented art work as a legacy of her true meaning and expression of her life on this planet.

Gone too soon, but see you on the other side my sweet friend, BIG Love, Lisa x (Co-author with Mich, Vols 3 & 5)

"Rattled Awake" was privileged to feature Michelle's artwork, personal journey and evolution. As Lisa put it,

"She was just getting started."

The ripples she left will become the oceans of memories we carry for the most humble, yet influential woman anyone could hope to call a friend.

"IT'S ONLY WHEN WE TRULY
UNDERSTAND AND ACKNOWLEDGE
OUR LIMITED TIME ON EARTH THAT
WE WILL BEGIN TO LIVE EACH DAY TO
THE FULLEST, AS IF IT WERE THE ONLY
ONE WE HAD."

ELIZABETH KUBLER-ROSS

Michelle did the artwork for this book, which has been the most popular book out of 13, so far.

She knew how to make emotions leap off the page.

"It's about the squiggles, Lonnee!

That's my personal touch. It's all about the squiggles!" she said with a giggle.

This colorful digital book showcases Michelle's art, process and incredible results: Rattled Awake: Volume Three in, "She's All HeArt…by Michelle Laaks"

After processing so much 'family stuff' she said, "Lonnee, I *need* to do another chapter with you." The title is who she became, a woman with pure JOY living a life with *NO Regrets*. This became her passion, her forever mission. You can read it here: Rattled Awake: Volume Five

HER TRADEMARK SQUIGGLES

Michelle, I swear it was, came to me on the day of her transition, while I stood outside crying. "Don't cry Lonnee! It was time to go. I'm fine! I'm right here. Please share my messages." Now you know how this book came about...

She did this one for me, so it seems fitting to close with it here. I hope to be like you someday, Michelle. You were my anchor and my buoy, my confidante and curious companion, exploring conspiracy theories together.

I hope you exited the matrix. Nonetheless, you are deeply missed here...

**Lonnee Rey** is dedicated to featuring the voices, and illuminating the people, who leave us both speechless and inspired. Reach out to her for a complimentary session about your book, or, to join in the movement of voices who refuse to be speechless any longer. Fnd her on LinkedIn, or visit: BookLonnee.com

# AFTERWORD

"Be who you are and say what you feel because
those who mind don't matter, and those
who matter don't mind." -Dr. Seuss

We learn from others' real world experiences. It is why
sharing our stories matters so much. Michelle Laaks went
too soon, but her legacy lives on in books.

Taking a chapter from your life is enough to make a
huge difference to people you may never meet, but who
desperately need to know you...to know how you made
it...whatever 'it' is.

Are you thinking about 'it'? Share 'it' before it's too late.

I believe you have lived to tell about it...*literally.*

*With Love,*
*Lonnee Rey, Editor*